sacred / profane

Edited by Gemma White

sacred / profane
Issue 1
Published by Only Words Apart Press
Copyright © 2013.

Copyright of the works published in this journal belongs to the author. Except for the purpose of fair dealing, no part of this publication may be reproduced without prior written permission from the publisher. Opinions expressed in sacred / profane are those of the contributors and not necessarily those of the editor or publisher.

Email: owapress@hotmail.com
Web: www.owamedia.com
Facebook: www.facebook.com/OnlyWordsApartMedia

ISBN 978-0-9874693-0-4
ISSN 2201-4446

Editing and Book Design:
Gemma White

Illustrations (inside and cover):
Tamar Dolev & Tara Patwardhan

Contents

Foreword

Thoughts & Writings
A Living Jewel	Richard James Allen	1

Poetry
Permit Holders	Alice Allan	2
Chimera	Richard James Allen	3
Home, Sweet Home	Richard James Allen	4
A Less Painful Surrender	Janette Ayachi	5
Something To Blacken The Paper	Janette Ayachi	8
The Skateboard	Stuart Barnes	10
On Your Engagement	Andrew Bifield	11
a thousand hats	Ashley Capes	13
Hangover	Louise Carter	14
Nan	Louise Carter	15
Reunion	Louise Carter	16
mother language	Dharmavanam Daws	18
Ugly	Alex Dowthwaite	19
First Chair	Rose Drew	21
The Feature Balks	Rose Drew	22
Seashell And Dialogue	Robert Drummond	23
Fuck Poem	Robert Drummond	25
The Red Hat	John Egan	26
Clinical Tastes	Bronwyn Evans	27
A Middle-Aged Man Dreams	Mark Farrell	28
Evenings	Michael Fitzgerald-Clarke	29
In Absentia	David Francis	30
Journey	David Francis	31
My Girlfriend	David Francis	33
Bearings	K.E. Fraser	34
A Universal Wish	Boris Glikman	35
Sunday Is Laundry Day	Nick Hadgelias	37
A Century Is The Drunken Blink Of An Eye	Barrie Hardwick	38
I Had The Best Sleep Of My Life In A Bank	Barrie Hardwick	40
Haven	Max Harris	41
Fluidity	Tim Heffernan	42
Listen	Tim Heffernan	43
Night Vision	Tim Heffernan	45
4 Bullets	Mark William Jackson	46

This Is Not For Valentine's	Mark William Jackson	47
Cemetery Visit	Marissa Johnpillai	48
A Patient Tells Me What's Missing	Debbie Lee	49
Crab Legs With Beer	Aurora M. Lewis	50
Moving On	Initially NO	51
Rising	Darryl Price	53
This Is Not Your Poetry	Darryl Price	54
Three Sentences Adding Up To One Spectacular Disease	Darryl Price	56
Mirror, Mirror Shoulder	Van Roberts	58
Willunga	Autumn Royal	59
Superproduct	Paul South	60
Things To Do In Moreland	Paul South	61
In The Corners	Ben Walter	63
Sweaters And Sunday Brunches	Wardenisms	65
A Coming	Paul Williamson	67
The Peak & The Eclipse	Deborah Wu	69
Contributor Biographies		71

Foreword

Before the idea for one journal called *sacred / profane*, I was originally going to publish two separate journals, one with a theme of blasphemy and one with a theme of the sacred. But then fate intervened, and a serendipitous conversation with Paul South (whose poetry is contained in this journal – see pages 60-61) about the nature of profanity and its innate connection to the sacred changed my plans. It seemed to me I was creating a false dichotomy with my separation of poems into two journals. Why separate what is two sides of the same coin? Why try to simplify what is inherently complex? It seemed to make more sense to mix it all up – one journal expressing the vicissitudes of life; the pleasures, the horrors, the transcendent moments – all in all, life's chaotic mystery.

It has taken a while to get this first issue together. I humbly thank all the poets published herein for their continuing patience with me. I hope to bring some more people on board Only Words Apart Media for the next issue, in order to lessen turnaround time. But withstanding hold-ups and a massive workload, it has been a pleasure to put this publication together and especially to find such evocative and sincere yet subtle and profound writing from poets in Australia and abroad.

Happy reading,

Gemma White.

Editor
sacred / profane
Only Words Apart Press

A Living Jewel

Richard James Allen

What is the soul? Someone asked me that question this week and I found it difficult to answer. There are so many definitions from different traditions and yet all seem to melt into intangibility when we try to pin them down. I am reminded of standing in front of a display case of exotic butterflies as a child, delighting in the swirling patterns of beauty in their wings and yet being saddened by their stillness and humbled at my inability to grasp their true nature which I could only imagine to be flight.

How often do we even ask ourselves such esoteric questions? Our days are filled with a chaotic rush into the future and the complex and often unspoken burdens of the past. We are overwhelmed by our habits of fear and desire, preoccupied with the pattern of our expectations and assumptions. And so we forget or put aside such things. Our attention is not brought to that which we cannot see, taste, smell or touch. And yet occasionally there passes through our consciousness the sense that we have a connection to something more powerful than anything we can so grasp.

And in these motionless moments, away if only for an instant from the spin of the world, we know that there is something beyond our marvelous but mundane sensing apparatus. Because we can feel it. Because in a strangely intuitive way we can hear it. It feels like the memory of movement. And it sounds like the beating of wings. It is the humming of the hovering of something which is beautiful but can never land – which is our soul.

This awareness, which varying cultures might call any number of things, precedes any particular religious or spiritual, creative or scientific, namings of it. This awareness, in a world of relativity, is a living jewel.

Permit Holders

Alice Allan

Monkeys don't remind anyone of Japan
but they are there,
watching the cars move past
from treetop vantage points.

Once, driving home from Katsurao
my friend saw a whole family
cavorting up the slope.
I was probably in Namie,
finding fat blossoms under snow.

That weekend we would have had too much to drink
and talked too loud about nothing
for too long.
Sunday the surfers would be grinning on the beach
and I'd try to think of more ways
to sew myself to this quiet green coast.

Now the beach, Katsurao, and Namie
are only accessible to permit holders.
You don't need to wear
the full disposable suit anymore,
but you can only stay inside the zone
for a maximum of three hours.

I guess the monkeys wonder
where all the cars have gone.

Chimera

Richard James Allen

when I think of God I find myself forgetting what I was going to say
as if the experience is too powerful for me to hold onto
the total data stream too dense to be assimilated
like a kind of heavy water that must be
evaporated leaving only a mist
with no more substance
than the wisps
of a

Home, Sweet Home

Richard James Allen

I'll come home later
and slip into something comfortable
I'll slip into you

A Less Painful Surrender

Janette Ayachi

Under the theatrical light of the upper gallery
I upheave your words, I start to remember how
you gave them to me, on the back porch
of the girl we both loved in different ways,
you flipped your chair to face mine, then placed
them in my hand like an offering of wine or flowers,
the sunset crowning you, your smile absorbing
                            the broken rays.

I lost those words soon after, buried them under
heavy time, light dust, many seasons' scattered leaves,
to only let them resurface when I heard about your death.
They bobbed like a bottle tossed to sink,
coughed up from the larynx of the guttural sea,
so I swam through waves of shadow to reach them
and the moon told me of your less painful surrender.

Reading the poems you wrote a few years before
your unsuccessful grapple with death, I sense
that you predicted your fall, and like any man
inherent of prophecies you did not fear the unknown
passage; a vermillion thrust of thwarted pansies,
the blue moonlight across your knuckles, the cage
of kestrels that opened in your chest with the last
                         cleaving thud of your heart.

But you never guessed what you would surrender,
painless or in agony, you never knew what you let go of
to leave, that sleeping child who could fill any crevice
or alcove of emptiness with his tiny breath, and that girl
linking us, who would have throned you her thunderbolt King.
But who am I to judge accidental overdose or suicide,
I am just the girl you met once, you shared no secrets
                       and no lies, only your poems

in which you wrote that you would rise again, resurrect
with your soul and I believe that sometimes when she needs
you, or sometimes when you have not touched her thought
in days, she feels you feather light against her cheek.
Even when you were alive you skipped across arcs of stars
for her, reservoirs of love poured, consumed and spiritualised.
Your syntax stabs at healed wounds, renders tears, as it reveals
            that only in your death was she able to live her years.

Something To Blacken The Paper

Janette Ayachi

Can anyone hear the earth move
or is it just the clouds that cry so loud
in the silence of the night?
Can you bear to carry the weight of our woes
when really all we have are tenacious flows
of light perhaps, as dark
proves not to be visible in a charnel hidden
with desires forbidden?
I take you in, I take your hand
which is warm against the ice of my skin
but deeper still I usher you within
by the echo of our laughs
we press our bones into the concrete
taking swifter inhalations of each other
under cover simply impostors
like the extinct animals of the jungle
nothing left but the food we survived on
growing on for another lover.
Stars adhesive against the backdrop of melody
the one between your legs perhaps
as I catch sight of your gross intuitions
something in the glass of your eye
that pulls me into your skull
where thoughts rotate and propel
like the engines of Earth and the Underworld.
Why is our connection always filtered
why do trees cry fire when it's only your tongue
that soothes me in a kingdom without words
and we are mute mothers who have left their
children in the wombs of their fathers
of ethereal light that is until we meet again
and sow our separate qualms
into the fabric of a flag we continue
unmarked by our predecessors
although we branch babbling into forests

we built together to salute our Gods
who rest fathoms below our subconscious
still gossiping about Joan of Arc.
So here now as the river opens and flood
gates no longer hold the Truth
a razor light sheds through the milkshake mist
African sister I am your blood
I bounce from the North to sever the flood
against the arid shores of Reason.
I see Algeria now she makes me hear the music
she makes me shy
but I sacrifice myself to the Sahara
and bring forth an oasis of labyrinth gardens
as my spirit pulls me towards the Northern Lights
and here comes the fire flies
like fireworks for the ants
but was it not the serpents
who showed you the way to me.
Spine to spine our skeletons intertwine
over the mouth of glass and steel
still I dream of hotels in Paris
of carrying exotic flowers
through the plazas of Florence
maybe then my hair will be grey.
Yet the leaves undress before me foliage flirting
and the night puts on her best lingerie
a red lace sunset with diamante planets pearls
that fashion her body the way
the Marquis de Sade fashioned his young girls
still I swagger through these vacant realms
my pockets of mind brimming with coined visions
and a gypsy girl asks me if I am lost
and I tell her that every sign post has directions
she winks at me like the landscape
and skips back into her fog playing the violin
in a coven with her sisters singing
to the dragon that sleeps in his cave
awaiting the vengeful sword
from melancholy to madness
I turn off the moon.

The Skateboard

Stuart Barnes

My god it was bloody
ugly: a zeppelin of a thing

hot pink wheels
a skull so dull I've

never
since feared death.

Especially at ten I loved history:
longed for the Place de la Concorde

to ring, for Brandenburg Gate
to uncage.

But I only ever hit
the yellowing brick

besieging a backyard's concrete
– the sound more gruesome

than thunderclaps rifling
this morning's chiaroscuro.

On Your Engagement

Andrew Bifield

Just think; a weatherboard, eaten by the indifferent salt air,
With the grass overgrown out front,
And a tangle of bikes, instruments and papers;
The taped front window; and compare

A well constructed marital home where
Amenity conveniently parks.
        That fortunate ——
That you're engaged to now – just contrast

His bricks and mortar finance role
With frustrated authorship, odd jobs, and the dole;
See what we could have had:
        At last,

Lying in bed with the lights out and our hangovers on
And a bottle of wine – dying
Young together.

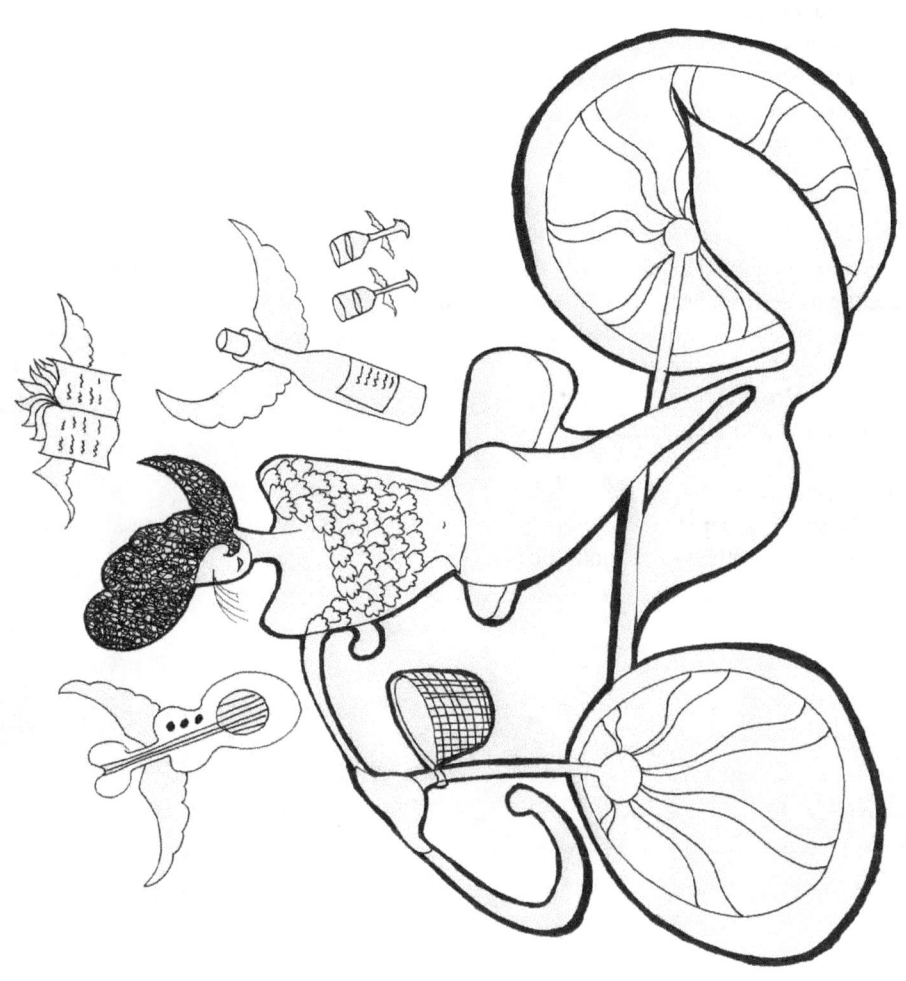

a thousand hats

Ashley Capes

you wait on a rust-covered footpath
for June to rush in
and upstage autumn
with a click of blue fingers and breath
that pulls frost over windshields

a grey-matter sky
between jingle jangle branches,
where someone has brushed in black clouds
you've been in a coffee house
and you're thinking about
getting away from here

not just winter, but the whole
year – you're thinking
nothing's worth going back for
and I'm struck by trees
like scarecrows lining up for orders,
hands groping after hats
the wind has scattered in a thousand places.

Hangover

Louise Carter

He only ever calls me drunk,
this man I once thought I loved,
back when I was young enough to think
that what we had was mystical and unique.

"It's so good to hear your voice!" he insists
in between sips. Of course it is.
He's called to declare his love,
for the umpteenth time in six years,
a statement which loses its appeal
with each slurred reiteration.

My unfinished poem stares back
accusingly from the screen,
appalled by how low I'll sink
for a distraction. But he's a very
complimentary monster, and my ego's
pathetically in need of feeding.

"You're brilliant," he says. "Extraordinary."
"Thank you," I reply with futility –
a previous version of myself
would have died instantly
of bliss, but it's too late now,
the moment's disappeared,
and the notion that I've been waiting
all these years in the hope he'd maybe one day ring
is more than a little insulting.

A muffled sound in the background
indicates he's been sprung. I hang up,
he calls back twice, but I leave him to
the hangover known as his life,
while I contemplate the bullet
that was nearly mine.

Nan

Louise Carter

"I don't like" is my Nan's favourite phrase
followed by "nothing spicy." Her hobbies
include watching the afternoon light
creep slowly across the wall and doing
my sister's laundry. She worries constantly
about what can't be controlled,
and I figure she's lived this long simply
out of suspicion that somebody somewhere
is doing something noncompliant.
There's a limit to how long I can listen
to her describe the correct procedure
for washing double sheets, so I begin
the convoluted process of trying to leave.
After the routinely laborious back and forth
she eventually sets me free;
the sun's trailing its way toward evening
and the rose-pink paint in her living room
has never looked more riveting.

Reunion

Louise Carter

He springs out from a crowd of tourists, buskers
and homeless people to hug me; he's early.

More than a year since I've seen him; the universe
has provided and retracted in equal measure.

It's windy, sunny, Sydney. Circular Quay's a mosh
pit, and the Botanical Gardens are overrun with

couples and parties and picnics and children.
We sit in the damp cold shade of a large tree,

the air carrying the unpleasant whiff of fertiliser,
and he tells me he wouldn't have made it here,

if not for the recently-discovered fact he's allergic
to sleeping pills. Spring cuts like a wound through

winter; knives of sunlight chopping the sea.
A boat out on the harbour wobbles dangerously.

"Do you think it'll capsize?" I ask. "I hope so,"
he says, blue eyes smiling in his lined face, hair

streaked with grey. He tells me of his journey
to Hobart and back – of sleeping rough, stealing

food from supermarkets, and getting lifts from
lonely truckies. He took LSD in Melbourne, gave

his spirit to the wind, and got his face smashed
in by drug dealers. Now he's back in my city

making coffee occasionally, still writing amazing
poetry that few will read. I loved him once;

considered being his wife; spent a night entwined

in a Buddhist temple that time after his mum died,

made love to him in my car on that heated night
when we clung to the backs of each other's pain

like parasites, only to wind up concussed
on the banks of experience, life paths severed

like car accident victims who rise from their wrecked
seats and walk away without looking behind them.

mother language

Dharmavanam Daws

the rite: pre-existent sounds incarnate
on lips amorous to their imperishabilities

a sonic relationship reconciles opposing principles
heart-fecundated, vowels rise on open tongue

alive in Devi's mouth, we play breathless
kirtan, setting the mood of dominant reds

magnifying our instrument's exquisiteness
tuned to the beginning of something vast

lokas follow a syllable shift
dew-plumped Her hibiscus fills the room.

Devi: Mother Goddess; luminous nature of spirit in its female aspect
Kirtan: chanting of mantras with musical accompaniment
Lokas: worlds or planes of consciousness

Ugly

Alex Dowthwaite

Ugly ugly ugly ugly, it's the 3AM hollow eyed ugly,
It's the sick CO_2 drunk nightmare ugly.
It's the street lamp traffic light ugly-
click click clicking for nobody but me.
It's the mushroom hobo church ugly,
It's the all time wrinkled no dime ugly.
It's the passing out in the alley
with your dick out and your head bleeding ugly.
It's the bucket bongs, rage, 4AM melted ice cream ugly.
It's ugly, alright, ugly fucking ugly.
It's dreams of inevitable death in the mating circus ugly.
It's up town low down ugly,
It's all the pretty girls and pretty drugs ugly.
It's the too high between two thighs ugly.
It's the moloch cement eternity ugly,
It's the warehouse poison industrial ugly.
It's the all American all consuming ugly,
It's the skin ointment dissapointment ugly,
It's skeleton junkies dying in the fetal position ugly,
It's the pretty plastic painted on people ugly.
It's shotgun ugly; the real ugly, the big ugly, the grey ugly.
It's the ugliness of the soul, burning alone
and once and for all in the selfish
narcotic angst of amphetamine dreams.
It's the ugliness of the mind,
numbed in the void of alcohol, marijuana and time.
It's the ugliness of the body, machine limbs burning
under the white heat of your eyes.
All is ugly.
Beauty is ugly.
Ugliness, this is it.

First Chair

Rose Drew

She can be gracious, graceful, unassuming, diffident,
a bitch: the rest of the flute section hates her.

You, the listener, have no clue,
as you watch her raise flute to poised pout,
and spill forth beauty, in vibrato.

You've no idea the politics involved
in an orchestra's flute section,
or even better, the machinations required
to reach First Chair.

The opening notes are played:
solo of course,
trembling in angelic purity.

The second row stares daggers
at her exposed spine.

As for the conductor?
It takes exceptional ears
to hear potential.

The Feature Balks

Rose Drew

But—there's no one here.
I look around me, reasonably convinced that we,
all six of us, do exist in time and space:
we are here.

But no, to our twice-cancelling
long anticipated Feature,
our scant few numbers do not begin
to represent a proper audience.
*I worked on this **all afternoon.***
I expected people to be here. I can't go on!

If she wants me to protest, I fail her.
If I am expected to ask her *please oh please*
to stay, she waits in vain.
I smile beatifically.
I nod with a nurse's pity. How sad. *Go on.*
She does, gliding off between
endcaps of best sellers,
calendar displays, travel guides.

We wait, tensely, as patpatpat her crêpe-soled
Hush Puppies carry her safely away
from our motley humbleness.
A Too-Small Poetry Gathering: that's new?

                                              we wait,
'til we can't stand it—
                                              is she gone?

then bust out laughing,
the street gang she had feared,
rightly;
our commonness revealed.

I'm sorry—your question again, oh yes:
why we don't have monthly features at our open mic?

Seashell And Dialogue

Robert Drummond

From the 13th beach sand hills
                      her correspondence on blue lined paper
attached to a striped shell, and scribbled alongside
her perfect signature   *p.s. can we reconcile?*
and once said that her soul
knew my soul
            but in cloudy moments
wanted (my soul)
                to swim up to conciousness,
to mouth a more easily digested vocabulary,
attempt at least to speak words that this day requires;
but on afternoons like this
my soul remains hidden,
                    and a harsh grammar
white hot with metaphor
unravels
       so close to home.

Fuck Poem

Previously published on the CD accompanying *Going Down Swinging*, number 18.
Robert Drummond

It's not fucking on mate -
        What's not fucking on?
That fucking arsehole was fucking supposed to fucking bring
along some fucking money.
                I'm fucking broke. I've got sweet
fuck all, so
no fucking drinks to-fucking-night.
                  You fucking sure?
Fuck oath I'm fucking sure, he's fucked it up.
Well fuck me,
      what are we going to fucking do?
Well, I'm fucking off back fucking home,
you can please your fucking self.
              You must be fucking joking.
Listen mate I've had more fights than feeds or fucking fucks,
would I be fucking joking?
              Well fuck off then,
go fucking home, fuck you and fuck your fucking joint,
I'm staying fucking here.
Ah go and get stuffed get nicked get fucked, I've never heard so much
fucking bullshit.
You are fucked, fuckface.
I'm fucked?
Fucking hell you're fucked, fuckface.
Well fuck me
you fucking arsehole, you are starting to fucking shit me.
Yeah, fuck you too, you fucking dickhead. What you need is a good fuck.
Where do you get a good fuck around here?
Don't fucking ask me, ask fucking them.
Don't tell me what to fucking do.
I'll tell you anything I fucking like, fuckhead.
Ah fuck,
fuck it.

The Red Hat

William Frater, 1937, The National Gallery of Victoria.
John Egan

A white dress, a cream jacket,
a young woman, hands on hips, seated, yes,
but leaning forward – her pale skin,
dark eyes and neat black hair, face aslant,
turned towards the light but her eyes
are searching yours.

The red hat dominates her face,
a flow in bold slashed across the forehead,
dipping almost to cover her right eye,
a sinuous flow of soft, of velvet,
a curve and dome and slope of red.

Lina Bryant, twenty eight,
assertive, determined and the red hat,
cherry red that flames from monochrome,
cherry lips and cherry scarf,
the red of luxury,
temptation, death.

You wore your own red hat for me,
playing at a gangster's moll
as I'd asked you to,
mouthing tough, spitting the words.
Dark eyes, black cascades of hair,
your eyes were searching mine.

You wore black stockings and gloves,
as I'd asked you to,
high heels, nothing else.
A famous painting, an antique hat,
Lina died at sixty one,
and you wearing a red hat for me,

naked in a moment of almost
make-believe, almost truth.

Clinical Tastes

Bronwyn Evans

Chamomile Tea
    burnt lips
    scattered cups paced away from misplaced
    dry mouth and the disappointment
    of flowers

Melting Moments
    they would give these to the patients
    keep them fat and happy
    small pleasures make time pass
    unwrapping them an easy routine to swallow

Soya Sauce
    smell the taste of salt
    imagined on a dim sim
    from the bain-marie
    in the café outside bland

Peppermint Stick
    lump in an envelope
    delivered by a nurse
    a green vial

    peppermint remedy rescue
    sent all the way from Australia

    something of my own
    personal
    something of you
    on foreign skin

A Middle-Aged Man Dreams

Mark Farrell

In the dream he is visited at home
by high-school friends he has not seen in years.
Decades ago they had created a zine that ran for sixty issues
and now they are trying to track down
each and every one of those issues.

The man is sure he doesn't have any
threw all his old things out
(or his wife did)
a long time ago.

His friends have a few copies of the zine with them though
and the man, curious, flips through a couple.
Ei-yi-yi! – cringe-worthy stuff:
clunky collages...
first-person diatribes in verse and prose...
crudely-drawn, unfunny cartoons...
limericks...

"Why do you want to visit the past
when the work is so bad?" The man asks.
"That is not the point," they tell him.
"But none of us became anything, or rather
none of us made it as a writer," the man continues.
"That is definitely not the point," they tell him.
"Then what is the point?" He asks.

"We are collecting something beautiful;
innocence, hope and ambition
preserving it so that such things do not leave the world."

And with that the man wakes up
goes to work
the dream, by lunchtime
forgotten.

Evenings

Michael Fitzgerald-Clarke

Our damaged humanity,
this temporal, fragile, earthly life.

In the dark evening
your songs have a wildness.

Your withdrawal, reticence,
the senses I gather from it

lead me to another dark evening,
fragile and gone.

I looked at your starry face then,
when you smiled and held me.

In Absentia

David Francis

I learnt a word

      from each woman

           that I loved

so many words

      each a story

           but never a poem.

Journey

David Francis

*'You leave me hanging by the skin of my teeth,
I've only got one leg to stand on
You send me to hell,
But I'll never let go of your hand'* - Tom Waits

We walked out one day
along the beach
as time passed
you came within reach
your body tanned
and wet on the sand
and I never let go of your hand.

I promised you then
I'd be there for you
'til death do us part
'til the bones show through
while making a stand
in our promised land
I never let go of your hand.

When the tide was high
you were caught at sea
in the undertow
you didn't see
the rut of a man
with his cunning plan
but I never let go of your hand.

I threw you a line
when you started to drown
I lost all hope
as the sun went down
but you called and I ran
like the beggar I am
and I never let go of your hand.

Now death's coming round
and we're soon to be dust
there's iron in the soul
but mettle can't rust
it wasn't what we planned
not nearly so grand
but I never let go of your hand.

My Girlfriend

David Francis

She wore her BA (Women's Studies)
like a pearl around her neck
hanging between her tiny breasts.
If she'd had a Masters or PhD
or bigger breasts
maybe she would have punished me less
for not being able to satisfy her.
Women with large breasts made her anxious
and angry for she believed they had the key
that unlocked a man's secret dream.
If she'd had a Masters or PhD
or bigger breasts
maybe she would have made love
instead of just fucking.
She said she wanted to try lesbianism
but couldn't kiss another girl
especially one with bigger breasts.
After she left me she became an earth mother
sensitive to everything, even to the flutter of a bird
in pain, but not to my pain.
Then she engaged in radical feminism,
had a stint with the Greens
tried yoga, reiki and tai chi,
graduated in acupuncture and danced with Sufism,
went through Buddhism,
and took up with a Hare Krishna,
but finally she found her true and natural calling
in black magic and witchcraft.

bearings

K.E. Fraser

floating, I face old familiar waves as they depart
the ocean's pull rolling on unchartered
drawing me steadily inside the sea
I am without importance or place
without history or template to guide
I do not matter out here where unending vastness is the norm
knowledge of land or friendship cannot complete
no-one keens to hear my last thought, my final desire

I slip beneath weightless quiet, my name already gone
distance folding out beyond the theatre of senses grown sharp in air
memory stills, captured
in the muted timbre of this holy, watery Om
falling strange and sweet and up and out
love's de-winged hummingbird unbounded by bliss

no stifled cry for life or help
the remnants of loss and regret set sail
a last coveted breath glitters into the velvety cold
breaking the surface of this ordinary existence
what remains is pulled into the depths of this tide exquisite
I hear a language writ large with a galaxy of starfish
as the moon of a whales tender love-song rises unmistakeable
from within the fathomless depths of every heart

A Universal Wish

Boris Glikman

It is the middle of a fresh December day.

I'm alone in the front yard,
building a snowman,
when the whole universe
lands beside me.

I can see myriads of
stars, galaxies,
clusters and superclusters
whirling inside it.

The blackness of its oceans of emptiness
contrasts sharply
with the whiteness of the snow.

I examine the Universe,
trying to solve
that age-old vexing question
of whether it is infinite or not.

I search for a maker's label
listing the Universe's specifications:
dates of manufacture and expiration,
gross and net weights, its exact ingredients,
but alas, the tag is nowhere to be found.

It then occurs to me that,
out of all the people in the world,
the Universe has chosen
to land at my feet.

This must surely be,
and I don't think I'm being too
presumptuous in arriving
at this conclusion,
a sign of some significance

and a personal message,
the meaning of which,
while not as yet entirely clear,
is undoubtedly an auspicious one,
although the method of
communication is rather dramatic
and not very subtle at that.

But then a devastating thought:
what if this is the result
of a wish made for a Christmas gift
a few weeks ago.

I can not lie to myself and deny that,
in a moment of frivolous avarice,
I wished for the entire universe.

I remember well dreading the punishment
I would surely receive from my parents
for making the universe fall from the sky,
the evidence of which will be harder
to hide than that broken vase.

Sunday Is Laundry Day

Nick Hadgelias

There's an angel
sitting next to me
in the laundromat,
waiting for his robes to dry.
He appeared
bathed
in a terrible, blinding light.

An immaculate choir sang the prayer of Azariah
as he loaded a washing machine
with divine grace.
He discovered a rebellious red sock
hidden amidst his basket of glittering shrouds.

He flicked through a Watchtower.
I sat in silence
as the angel whistled a tune
ageless and strange.

The angel borrowed a dollar from me for the machine.
When my clothes were dry
they were bright and pure and gleaming
just as the box had promised.

A Century Is The Drunken Blink Of An Eye

Barrie Hardwick

She likes poems
about fish tanks
and snow. I am a
volatile poet and
cannot write of
such things. We

may never be
matched in any
universe. Elusive

bloody purpose.

Idly, I wonder
what I could
possibly be
leaving for
others. It'll

need to be
something
great. So they

can carry me in
their minds, in
their words and
on their walls.

Forever.

She'd notice
then.

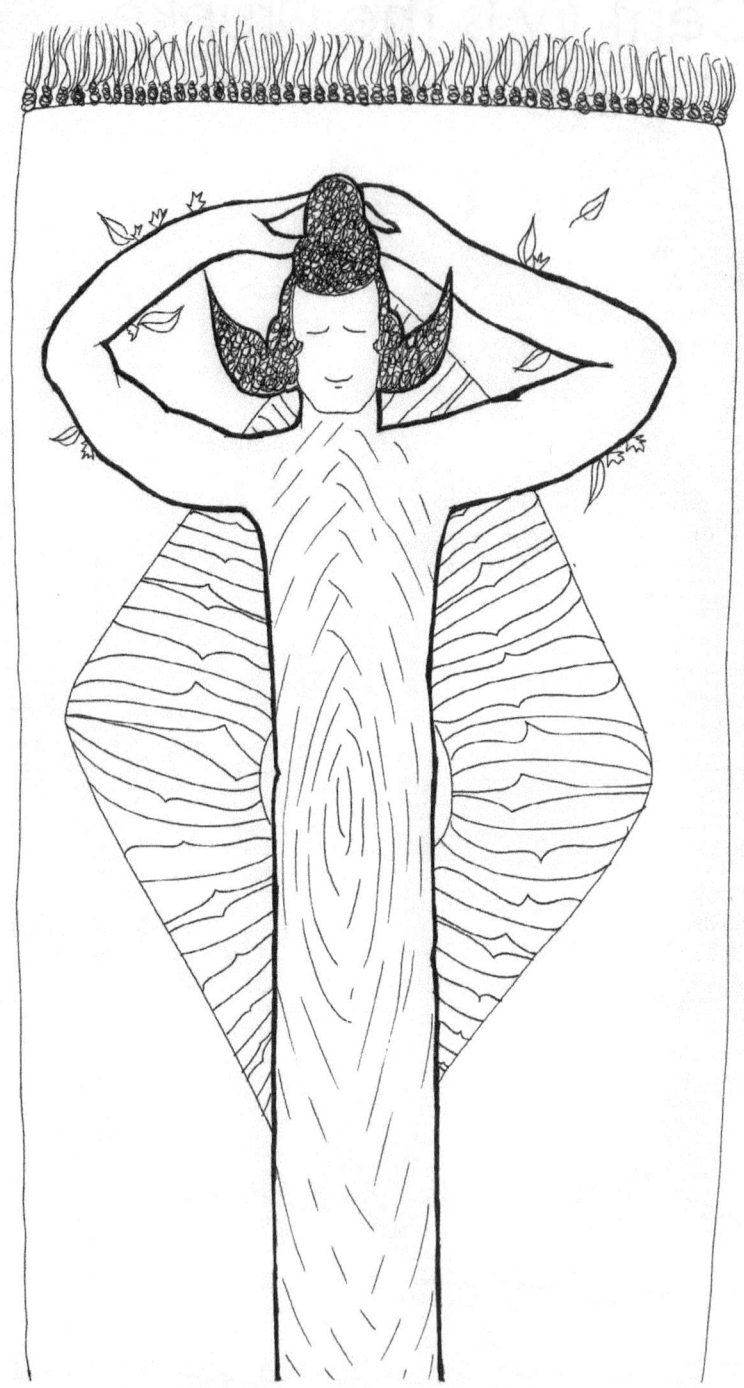

I Had The Best Sleep Of My Life In A Bank

Barrie Hardwick

warm air and smooth carpet
melancholy grey and simply beige

soft giggles of the pretty bank girls
float in the air
sat behind their genuine helpful smiles
as their tap tap tap computers
whirr gently

i close my eyes
a stamp, staple and an ambulance
streets away

paper being moved from pile to pile
pens scribble and printers hum

the rain outside
another ambulance
closer
this time

i'm in the softest seat i've ever sat in
i sleep as people queue
and the man next to me whispers a song

we are waiting.

Haven

Max Harris

Waves war with the desperate shoreline
gulls toss like origami in the wind.

The purple-red headland stands in conflict
with an unrelenting sea

it has stood rock solid for eons,
tempestuous days carve at its strength

a thousand savage blades
an unwinnable battle with the years.

Sky with a bellyful of rain
threatens a tearful foot stamping tantrum.

Lights go on along the slickened streets
to illuminate the impending deluge.

Workers rush to the reassurance of home.

Fluidity

Tim Heffernan

You went down to the water
You went to the water
You went to water

You went too close to the edge
You went to the edge
You went too close

Close to the water
Close to the edge
You went down to the water's edge

You edge closer

Listen

Tim Heffernan

Let them speak to you

of the madness of God while they
are psychotic deluded hearing
their voices frightened of you with
knives in their hands following
the wind pacing the street in
communion with traffic lights in
that lucid time when they are in
dialogue with their demon spirit
the one that leads them to those
other places

Let them speak to you

Night Vision

Tim Heffernan

Delusions of Messianic proportions had been revealed to him on several occasions when he had immersed himself in his manic disposition. He had begun with the words: recording the messages that flooded his mind. Swiftly symbols saturated and rented him from his social reality into a realm where he was to be Saviour and King. On several occasions the ambulance arrived with guardian angels who waved the magic syringe, depositing him for terms in starry-eyed wards where he was needled back from the heaven of his own creation. Still now, feet firmly planted in the elements – anchored by lithium – he often remembers his raving idea while looking at the stained soil of his same existence. At night when he once woke and walked guided he now sleeps in a marital bed and his dreams release the prescribed shackles. The idea remanifests and for the eternity of the vision his mission is revealed to the weary, waiting masses. Waking, he stumbles out and pisses into the ceramic reality that is the drain that will be his day. In the fogged head of morning remnants remind him that somewhere suffering has ceased and prophecy promises to resurrect each time he closes his eyes and lies suspended.

4 Bullets

Mark William Jackson

4 bullets and he is taken,
a day in a life that changed the world.

4 bullets from the shaky barrel of
a nowhere man and history explodes.

4 bullets and we can no longer imagine
there's nothing to live or die for.

4 bullets anonymously manufactured
that still ricochet today.

This Is Not For Valentine's

(Edited Version)
For Silvia, 2012.

Mark William Jackson

You aren't my whole smile,
but you are the corner of my eyes
that wrinkle once my mouth has
curled as far as it can.

You aren't my whole cake,
but you are the sweet crumbs
I collect by pressing my
finger to the plate.

You aren't my whole day,
but you are there when I sleep,
and you are there
when I wake.

You aren't my whole life,
but you are the reason
I am not merely
birth and end dates.

You aren't everything I love,
but you are the reason I know what love is.

Cemetery Visit

Marissa Johnpillai

I am drawn to this
gated community, plotted out
at a time when we'd had all the space
in the world to bury the dead.

From afar it's a graveyard
picnic, the whole town stretching
its lazy bones into a horizon
of blankets. Each family keeps

to their spot. But up close
it is cold. The cemetery sharpens
a pencil and tells me to hold
still. The cemetery slows

my heartbeat, sketches
the oval of my face, marks
lines for the angle of my nose,
eyes and mouth. The cemetery

kisses my lips, says *baby
don't you want me?*, shows me
angels with half-opened wings, the ends
of their fingers crumbling.

A Patient Tells Me What's Missing

Debbie Lee

In a stale communal room
I feel the flush on my cheeks.

Leaking eyes and clenched
hands wonder what is needed.

Outside alone and anxious
a patient tells me what's missing.

He is God.
But no-one loves him.

He wants a girlfriend.
Would I be his girlfriend?

A nurse tells the patient
to stop bothering me.

But I'm not bothered.
I'm disconcerted.

How could I tell him?
I don't believe in God.

Crab Legs With Beer

Aurora M. Lewis

Cold of night warmed by your smile
And the light that flickered within
Your eyes while strolling along the pier
Stopping to buy crab legs steamed and
Ice cold bottles of beer

Shielding me from
The whipping wind
Your beard tickling my face
Your laugh echoing in my ear
As you pulled dollars from nowhere

To share this treat as we waited
My hands in your coat pocket
To keep them warm
There was no need as my heat
Was always drawn from you

Cracking open the shells
Pulling the sweet warm meat
From broken limbs sucking the
Juices from separated legs
Lips sealed with kisses tasting of hops

Knowing you would hold me close
At the meal's end and soothe me
With the warmth of your skin
And the wave of lovemaking
Crashing to shore once more.

Moving On

Initially NO

Moving love's lament
And words wrongly sent to you
Whom I love too much.

Colourful beauty
I caught you with my eye-lid
In time's wrinkling.

I ripped the lace ring
That danced around your being
And flattered your ace.

I wish I said you
Were all I was thinking of
Tomorrow, sunshine.

Sun shines on beauty
Just as rain falls to grow more
I dig you so much.

How many words given
In thought of how much I love
Your weather today.

Rising

Darryl Price

The coin, so little, the watch chain, the youth,
so to speak, each hand, the panic room, the
here and there, the ashtray, the stumps, the distance now,
the feathers, the jump, the radiant shadows, the spine
in gold letters, the arc, the circumstances, the mirrors,
stories, the talk, the torn away grasses, the collective
nouns, the aesthetic, the city limits, the next year,
the correct use of the young money's predicament, the
voices, the hell, the hunting of the relevance of
the object, these boys, the light of the lamp,
the bonkers world, the baseball cap, the old pine trees,
the flapping din, by contrast, the most maddening
thing, the darkening apartments, brick, outside the window screen,
the lightning, fire, the strange smell, the endless appetite
beneath, biting the inside of my mouth, the small
lie, if you insist, the puzzled exaltation of rising.

This Is Not Your Poetry

Darryl Price

Your begging hands are like garden
claws that know not the difference
between a delicate
solar powered flower
and a tightening choke of
weeds. It's not like it's even
mine to keep - like a legal
document I'd give over
to you in some kind of forced
treaty. I wouldn't want to,
of that you can be sure. Oh
please don't name it wild and then
call it dangerous. You can
only pronounce correctly
what you will let live this time
around and all others too.
It always belongs to just
itself. Befriend the fact by
being as you are. You could
say I'm the latest modern
keeper but I'm not the only
lost one it will come to;
with its saintly seeking in
time it will prove its own powerful
freedom above all
else. It exists without you
and within you. I'm honored
to give it my own sad little
tongue, my caught in the trope
throat, a heartbeat to travel
along for sending a sonata
of eternal messages.
We all shall have our fleeting
agreements you could say with
this mysterious one's visits
like a sudden full moonlight
entering our fevered

dream-tents at night. It comes and
goes as it pleases but drops
a startling lustrous feather
or two my way (only) periodically;
these jewels I wear
in my own hair as a sign
of respect and solidarity.
But they will be
taken from me by the enemy
sooner or later.
They will kill me thinking they
have silenced a happy bird,
but angels will lift the difference
with their prayers and
nothing will be lost forever
except ignorant doubt
and restless fear. Peace is a
kind of beauty that surpasses
its own meaning and waits.

Three Sentences Adding Up To One Spectacular Disease

Darryl Price

1. Oh I'm just kicking around you could say I'm not waiting around anymore certainly not hoping to see if your free falling hair still looks like it belongs on no other perfected face more to the heavens more than to the earth tribes whatever I don't mean to talk about you at all there's a whole world relax you'll find something else to dive for and someone to do it with and yeah I've still got plenty of my pretty poems pouring like precious leaking blood rivulets ever so slowly oozing out of me so I don't need you to inspire me with your pitiful dancer's teeth a smile like that doesn't come from eating a chicken sandwich at your local you know what I mean that's the problem for me you always knew you got it and said so but you'll watch the leaves break until you get bored again bored with uneven sidewalks bored with rain scarves with broken hearted cars with bad movies on the backs of bad trailers inside and out oh there I go like I said you've got it all wrong and you've always had it there the whole time at your least beck but all you want is to rack up another cool thing you haven't tried to consume yet did you ever think about the price to others again doesn't matter I've seen you sway them they end up remorseful for being so foolish in the face of your unbelievable crushing beauty and you always smile as you kick them out of the moving car but I've never seen you turn your head back around and take a look someday when you do you're going to see a cave-in I suppose.

2. I don't need to count the stars I'm sure they go on forever or longer than I have time to care or matter while you'll be invited to each new heavenly discovery your name will be carved on stardust and used to dazzle mere mortals with a thousand bizarre dreams that they will never be able to forget some will collect names hoping to eventually find yours and then say it shout it over and over again until every bell has been rung every last song has been drained of its music every built stairs have been climbed and now there is no need only you'll be at the bottom waving bye see you next time or never how about we just say never and let it go at that you can't expect to go where I am after all I am the key and a key will travel through a lock every time that's all you don't have to cry it's not about you it's about travel that's all my feet cannot curl up for long isn't that how you put it while he waited in the next room holding a chair and a cushion casting his shadow on your back like a net while you collected the tears that would later be turned into some awfully fast cash the kill would be his blame to bear alone and you leave history to the soft students and it's so easy to change your shoes into swans and glide away on a lake made of nothing more than the long locks of your hair like a lost highway that simply rolls up into itself and

pops off into nothingness like a firecracker like the first rain drop like the engine in the night that roars off into a million possibilities while you beg it wait wait wait for me please.

3. And so I'm still alive but feeling a bit like a surfer's washed up board with a big chunk bitten out of it the only thing anyone can do is speculate how big the creature must have been who targeted it but you you are completely disappeared and now the only reality you fit into is the one that is missing but well I find myself not so alone there are a lot of ghosts a lot more than you would ever have thought still this is no garden lost in another garden's ear it's a cold cold cold breeze that slaps these rocks with its heartless wind cranked hand but the beat is so monotonous but okay you don't want to hear this it's just no fun and without fun there's no colourful restaurants only sorrow and its stupid little children and with sorrow you need only one pair of pants I get it you were made for so much more but did you ever think of your hands digging in my dirt like a prayer what did you put in there why did you grow something in me if you weren't going to be around to take care of it how did I get to be the caretaker of something I'd much rather forget right now forever and yet I see that it needs me that it belongs in the world nothing asks for this kind of pain not even from your kind of hell and so I come here and let it fall into the pit of this poem it's all I can do it's all I want to do for you so if you don't mind here's your wedding gift may it bring you hours of utter silent happiness set among the other captured flowers.

Mirror, Mirror Shoulder

Van Roberts

"You again?"
the grim green of the '60s bathroom

                                                                      is hungry
                                                    is licking its chops

this morning.

                                                                     In its sights
                                                                        it floods

it dribbles over its canines
this morning.

The towel
flaps in the grim green of the rusty taps

                                              it scrapes cloven hoof
                                     it won't take no for an answer.

Willunga

Autumn Royal

A stinking, ant-plagued summer with slamming
doors and a howling mother,

her hairless daughters refusing to swallow
church, much preferring to construct cubby houses

with sandy slept-in sheets and sunburnt bricks.
An interruption is pulling on sun-smart costumes

and driving to Aldinga Beach, for little sister is only ever
happy bathing herself in the ocean's possibilities.

Screaming with wonder and then wondrous pain,
a fishing hook kisses and inserts into her pale foot,

waves tug, tug the hook's line and draw little sister
en route to an unprepared future.

Mother sits, helpless from divorce, and mourns
her own childhood war of cricket bats and nose-bleeds.

Like a cartoon mouse, big sister scurries to the rescue and
survival-strokes little sister to shore.

The hook is finally sucked out clean, and replaced with
realisations of role-play and tetanus.

Superproduct

Paul South

Sweeping the world like a pandemic
Felching the poorest corners of Bollywood
Free in packs of Cornflakes
For a limited time
Collect all 30 and win a Ferrari
Free radical baseball caps for the kids
Just SMS 'tumour' for your
Cancer like a horse's cock
Trembling through power grids
Fizzing overhead wires
Viral load to shut down web browsers
Nikkei going into noughts and crosses
Burns porn upon retinas
Rips bukkake like a haiku
Converts money into euros
Speaks Esperanto with pan American accent
Moves into the Kardashian house
Has a threesome with god and the devil
Download now for $5.95/min
Turns swamps into satellite suburbs
Fucks your default page settings
Photoshops behinds breasts
Voice modulates Guy Sebastian
Pulps and reincarnates as phrases
heard on mobile phones on trains.

Things To Do In Moreland

Previously published in *Rats Live On No Evil Star.*
Paul South

Buy umbrella from thrift shop.
Buy backpack from thrift shop.
Pick up dead pigeon.
Bury under the tree in Safeway car park.
Get egged by a car full of teenagers.
Write a poem about getting egged
      by a car full of teenagers.
Eat an over-ripe banana.
Stare at old Italian men staring at you.
Tell beggar you have no money.
Get dinged by a tram.
Meet Andy and bitch about poets.
Go to Brunswick Hotel
      and watch people get drunk.
Go to falafel joint at midnight
      and pack colon.
See Sydney Rd glazed in the wet.
Punch self in head
      just to feel something.
Clod along Merri Creek.
Piss behind the Willow tree.
Sniff fingers and look at the stars.

In The Corners

Ben Walter

falling for the Spring,
and dressing up as Autumn,
the blossoms drift on concrete steps, neither
illustrating nor imagining, they gather
in corners like rusted fruit,
pressing wrinkled pictures
of flushed youth
on diminishing companions.

Sweaters And Sunday Brunches

Wardenisms

On the bar stool in the kitchen
me
Burgundy
in the glass
on my lips
on her sweater

Her sweater
reserved for Sundays
her breasts under that sweater
screaming for liberty
on the Sunday
her breasts as plump
as the tomatoes
she's sliced
and diced
and thrown into the pan
with the hand of a chef
and the fingers of an artist

I could watch her for hours
and days and months and years
I could watch her
turn over bacon
make hollandaise
poach eggs
I could watch her
take off the apron
smelling of Sunday's brunch
and Dior

I could watch her
slide between my legs
slide a wedge of melon
into my stained mouth

and wait a moment
wait for me to chew
and swallow
before the kiss
on the stained lips
amidst the food
in the kitchen
on the Sunday.

A Coming

Paul Williamson

Who you are is not a mistake
not a mental lapse by providence.
The plan evolved
with complex care to form you
unique, for earnest tasks.
What makes you different
exactly why, is obscure
but you are called by name and chosen
not to be somebody other than you
but to become most fully you.

The Peak & The Eclipse

Deborah Wu

What I should have told you
before we came to climb the peak
and see the eclipse
is that you smell like whiskey
like my Grandpa.

On our way to the peak
to see the eclipse
We stopped to smell the roses
but all I could smell was
the whiskey on your breath
and on your jacket and on your neck
while descriptions of tigers floated
like apparitions in my head.

On our way to the peak
to see the eclipse
you dropped a five cent coin
a little echidna that no one else
would care for, or look at
or pick up
I thought it was two dollars
two whole dollars to buy me some wizz-fizz
or sherbet bombs or jelly snakes
I tucked it into my pocket just the same.

On our way to the peak
to see the eclipse
you stopped me and said
you had something to tell me
and I waited and thought
'but that's what you told me'
I bent down to tie my shoelace
and you said to never mind.

On our way to the peak
to see the eclipse
the moon had hidden behind some clouds

and you said 'bugger' and 'oh no
we're too late' so you stopped
and we perched
on the rock by the peak
and you kissed my mouth
while I looked at the saltbush scrub
and tried to think of how to get the stains out of my shoe.

On our way to the peak
to see the eclipse
you were happy with my hair
and the way it looked
in the moonlight
now that the clouds had gone away
and we could see the river running
and you laughed and said
we hadn't missed it
but we very nearly did.

What I should have told you
after we went and climbed the peak
and saw the eclipse
is that you smell like whiskey
like my Grandpa
who never really loved me.

Contributor Biographies

Alice Allan is a freelance writer, editor and poet based in Melbourne. Her work has appear in publications such as *Going Down Swinging, Australian Poetry* and *Cordite*.

Australian born Richard James Allen has published nine books as a poet, fiction, performance writer and editor, most recently *The Kamikaze Mind* (Brandl & Schlesinger). His writing has appeared widely in magazines, journals, anthologies and online. A multi-award-winning poet, performer, choreographer, film and new media maker, and scholar. www.physicaltv.com.

Janette Ayachi is a London-born Edinburgh-based poet with degrees from Stirling and Edinburgh Universities. She has published internationally across a wide range of print and online literary journals/anthologies including *Poetry Salzburg Review* and *New Writing Scotland*. Her pamphlet *Pauses at Zebra Crossings* was released last year and her second collection *A Choir of Ghosts* will be launched from Calder Wood press in April 2013. For further information and more poetry visit: www.janetteyachi.webs.com

Stuart Barnes lives in Cooee Bay, where he edits *PASH* capsule, an online journal of contemporary love poetry. He's currently working on Blackouts & other poems, a manuscript dedicated to the memory of Gwen Harwood, who encouraged the eleven-year-old him to write poetry. Poems are forthcoming in *Southerly*, blackmail press, *Mascara Literary Review, Establishment Magazine* (UK), & *Assaracus: A Journal of Gay Poetry* (USA).

An expatriate Western Australian, Andrew Bifield settled in Melbourne by way of London and, for a brief, strange time, the Northern Territory. He won the Written Word category of the 2012 Qantas Spirit of Youth Awards with a collection of his poetry.

Ashley Capes teaches Media and English in Victoria. He moderates online renku site 'Issa's Snail' and his poetry collection, *Stepping Over Seasons,* was released by IP in 2009. More recently, a haiku chapbook, *Orion Tips the Saucepan* was released by Picaro Press (2010). He occasionally dabbles in film and loves Studio Ghibli films.

Louise Carter is a Sydney-based poet whose work has appeared in *Best Australian Poems 2012, Trunk: Blood, The Green Fuse, The Sex Mook, Velour Zine,* and *Voiceworks*. She is currently working on her first collection, *Romancing the Mundane*. Her biggest literary hero is Helen Garner and she hopes to one day mentor young writers.

Dharmavanam Daws is now a Melbourne based poet & freelance writer after spending many years travelling as a wandering yogi, poet, musician, and improvisor. He has had poems and articles published in various local, national and international magazines and journals.

Tamar Dolev creates unique and fun artworks that take you into the imagination where anything is possible. In her current works she uses vibrant texta colours on paper, wood and cardboard. She also takes photos of the everyday little things in life that often go unnoticed. Tamar is currently studying art therapy where she hopes to assist people in their own journey through creativity. Please check out Tamar's website (www.tamardolev.com) or Facebook page (tamarART) for any enquiries about her art practice.

Alex Dowthwaite is a young, up and coming writer based in Melbourne. His favourite hobbies include traversing Congolese jungles with his young manservant, Mabutu, hunting wilderbeast on the plains of the Serengeti and smoking the finest oriental opium with Elizabethan scholars. Keep your ears open!

Rose Drew has hosted open mics in one country or another since 2003. She's found in *scissors and spackle, CT River Review, Fairfield Review, Strong Verse, The Machineries of Love* (Ragged Raven Press) among others. Her book, *Temporary Safety* made No 9 on 2011 Purple Patch 20 Best Individual Collections.

Robert Drummond's poems have appeared in many literary journals , including *Overland, Southerly, Going Down Swinging, Westerly, Poetry Canada, Eureka Street, Best Australian Poems 2008*, and he has read his poems at festivals, universities, and numerous other venues since before the dinosaurs vanished. A book of his poems *Ships On Fire* was published in 2002, and new book and performance cds are in the pipeline.

John Egan is a Sydney poet, who also spends a lot of time on the south coast of NSW. He is a retired teacher and his chapbook *Not the Rain, the Wind* is published by the Melbourne Poets' Union. He writes on diverse themes but they are usually related to personal experience, especially to memory and the sea.

Bronwyn Evans is an emerging Melbourne- based poet and short story writer. She has worked variously as a property valuer, chef and English teacher. She has one dependent named Smokey, an outdoorsy grey cat. Bronwyn runs a writers' group in Port Melbourne, Victoria. She is currently working on a collection of poetry.

Mark Farrell is from Nova Scotia, Canada and has been living in the Czech Republic for over fifteen years. He teaches at Charles University in Prague. His work has appeared in many journals throughout the world – most recently in *Nashwaak Review*

(St. Thomas University, Canada) and *Post Poetry Magazine* (London, UK).

In 2012 Michael Fitzgerald-Clarke launched *The South Townsville micro poetry journal* http://thesouthtownsvillemicropoetryjournal.blogspot.com.au/. It seeks poetry of all kinds that is twenty-five lines or fewer. When he's not burning the midnight candle responding to submissions, he's often running up his phone bill.

David Francis writes poems and short stories. His work has been published in *Verandah, Famous Reporter, Velour, Windmills, Rabbit* and *Unusual Work*. He works in Melbourne and Kathmandu as a transplant surgeon.

K.E. Fraser is a former Verandah editor with poetry remaining a constant companion and oldest friend. A degree in Writing and Anthropology has fuelled an addiction to observation and gratitude for connecting through words and cups of tea on the Everest climb that is writing and publishing.

Boris Glikman is a writer, poet and philosopher from Melbourne. The biggest influences on his writing are dreams, Kafka and Borges. His stories, poems and non-fiction articles have been published in various online and print publications, as well as being featured on national radio and other radio programs.

Nick Hadgelias is a writer and musician based in Melbourne. He is currently studying a Masters of Creative Writing, Publishing and Editing at Melbourne University. Nick has had a couple of poems published in Melbourne University's student magazine, Farrago and in online poetry publications. He has two very curious rabbits.

Barrie Hardwick is your typical friendly, bearded, t-shirt-wearing fella who's a fan of chilling out, cider and graphic novels. He scribbles words occasionally, and occasionally they shuffle themselves into an order that resembles a poem. They then, working as a team, climb onto pages of very decent poetry publications. Barrie lives in England.

Max Harris - not *the* Max Harris of Angry Penguins fame - is 69 years young. Born in Crookwell, New South Wales, he is now confined to a wheelchair. He belongs to the Arts Council Scribes Poetry Group in Hervey Bay, Queensland, co-ordinated by his very able wife Lynn.

Tim Heffernan made his literary debut in *The Wagga Daily Advertiser* in 1985. His poetry has also been published in *OZpoet, Thylazine, Cordite, Eureka Street* and Blackmail Press. He lives in Wollongong, NSW.

Mark William Jackson is a Sydney based poet whose work has appeared in various print and online journals including: *Best Australian Poems 2011, Popshot (UK), Going Down Swinging, Cordite, The Diamond & the Thief* and *SpeedPoets*. For more information visit: http://markwmjackson.com

Marissa Johnpillai is a poet who is burying her toes in Melbourne for a brief while. Hailing from the islands of Bermuda, Sri Lanka and Te Wai Pounamu (colloquially known as the South Island of New Zealand), she also writes songs, love letters and light-heartedly pleasant replies to rejection e-mails.

Debbie Lee, a widely featured writer on RedBubble, enjoys the possibilities of poetry and wordplay. She has performed from Ballarat to Brunswick, and in 2012 arrived in Brisbane. Debbie is happiest sharing food with friends and family, or eradicating rogue apostrophes from text. For more writing, please visit http://www.redbubble.com/people/msdebbie.

Aurora M. Lewis is a graduate of UCLA's Creative Writing Program. She is the recipient of an Honorable Mention in *Gemini-Magazine*'s most recent poetry contest. Aurora's work has appeared in *The Hatchet, Up the Staircase*, Vagbondage Press, *Wordgathering, Dreamers Reality, Watchtower Monthly*, as well as other publications.

Initially NO has a diploma in Professional Writing and Editing from RMIT. She has had poems published in *Positive Words Magazine, Taj Mahal Journal, Platform Magazine, The Ghazal Page* and has a number of books available from Amazon. She is also publishing a memoir about manic psychosis called *Naked Ladies*, with London's Chipmunka Publishing. It has poems as well as illustrations within the narrative. She is studying Art Therapy, but enjoys MCing West Word poetry and reading at many Melbourne venues in her spare time.

Tara Patwardhan sees the world as one big canvas. And all the beings in the world are different coloured paints. Her current inspiration comes from morphing unlikely pairs together. She does this to express the oneness and connectivity between all beings. For paintings, posters, table matts, greeting cards and more, email her at tarapatwardhan@gmail.com

Darryl Price was born in Kentucky and educated at Thomas More College. A founding member of L. Jack Roth's Yellow Pages Poets, he has published dozens of chapbooks, and his poems have appeared in many journals.

Van Roberts lives in Melbourne. She taught English in Mexico before returning to Australia and her love of words. Her poetry manuscript was shortlisted for the PressPress Chapbook Award 2010 and she also writes for her blog, Scribbley-Ness. Vanessa is part of Little Raven Publishing and is currently completing a Diploma in Professional Writing and Editing at RMIT.

Autumn Royal is a PhD candidate in literary studies at Deakin University, Geelong, where she is writing on the verse novels of Dorothy Porter. Autumn's work has appeared in *Antipodes, Lip Magazine, Rabbit Poetry Journal* and *Windmills*.

Paul South has been writing for 15 years, and has performed at literary events including The Melbourne Writer's Festival, The Fringe Festival and Words In Winter. Tragic and often comic, Paul's pieces have a disarming simplicity and directness that make him a crowd favourite. He has recently released a book of poetry and prose, *Rats Live On No Evil Star.*

Ben Walter is a Tasmanian writer and poet. His writing has appeared in *Famous Reporter, Overland* and *Island.* He is the editor of the recent award-winning craft/story collaboration, *I Sleep in Haysheds and Corners.*

Wardenisms prefers to remain an enigma.

Gemma White is a Melbourne-based poet, editor of *sacred / profane* and founder of Only Words Apart Media (www.owapress.com). Her work has appeared in *Voiceworks, page seventeen, Visible Ink* and *Award Winning Australian Writing 2011.* She writes poems that distil everyday moments in time, infusing them with meaning, sometimes adding a touch of the surreal or imaginary.

Paul Williamson has published poems in magazines including *Five Bells, Short and Twisted, Hands like Mirrors, This Next Wave, Eucalypt, Melaleuca, Tamba* and *Magic Cat* (UK). His poetry arrived after three research degrees (two in Science and one nominally in Arts but apparently in Sociology). He writes poems to try to clarify feelings and impressions, and then record them.

Deborah Wu is a first year university student with writerly aspirations. She writes short stories and poetry because she lacks the attention span to attempt anything more substantial. Last year she worked as a Provocateur with the Malthouse Theatre, chatting about inspiring theatre with inspiring audiences.

www.ingramcontent.com/pod-product-compliance
Lightning Source LLC
Chambersburg PA
CBHW070939160426
43193CB00011B/1744